Lao Consonants/Alphabets

ພາສາລາວ

Picture Book with English Translations

This is a beautiful book for children of ages 4+ to learn Lao Alphabets

A perfect Lao Consonants/Alphabets Book with Alphabet, Words and Pictures with English Translations.

- *The book details each of the 27 Lao Alphabets - CONSONANTS, the English phonetics, the commonly used word in Lao, its associated English word for easy understanding and reference with pictures.*
- *Picture book details all **27 Lao Consonants/Alphabet letters with 4 page per Alphabet** to practice writing and letter tracing along with **guiding directions on how to trace them***
- ***111 Black and White pages**, providing amble space for kids to practice letter tracing*
- *The book is created to help teach the alphabet to beginners. Arrows and dots are included to help teach the stroke order.*
- *Premium color cover design*
- *Printed on high quality perfectly sized pages at 8.5x11 inches Black and White pages*

Help us out

We are a small business, and your brief review could really help us. The following link will take you to the **Amazon.com** review page for this book

vapari.page/reviews/37

We appreciate your feedback & support, and sincerely hope to serve better.

Lao Consonants Alphabets/Letters

ພາສາລາວ

ກ ຂ ຄ ງ ຈ

ສ ຊ ຍ ດ ຕ

ຖ ທ ນ ບ ປ

ຜ ຝ ພ ຟ ມ

ຢ ຣ ລ ຫ ອ

ຮ ຮ

g

ไก่

gai

[Chicken]

First, trace following the directions; then repeat on the other prompts.

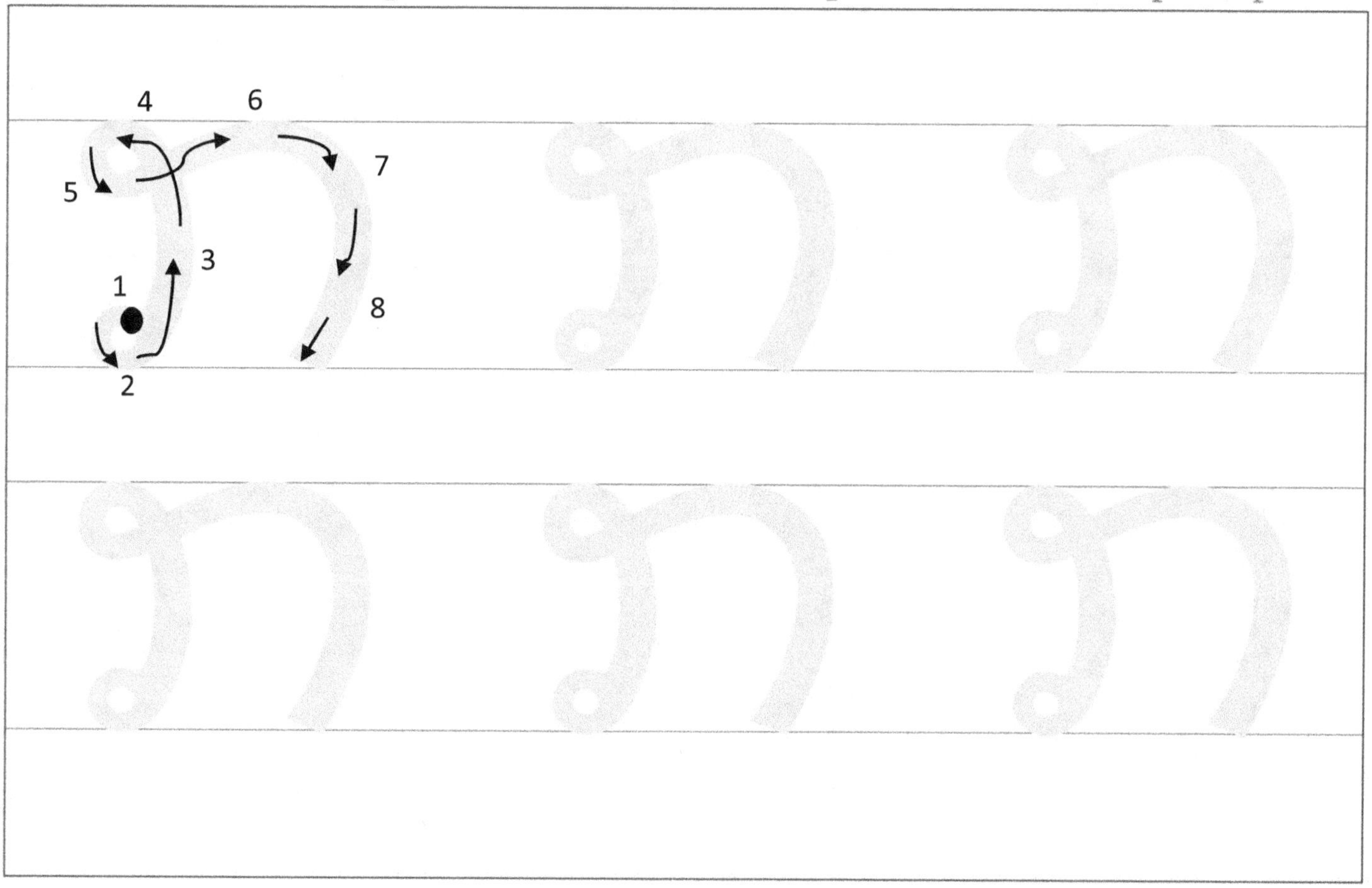

Practice repeating the letter by tracing over each prompt.

Practice repeating the letter by tracing over each prompt.

Practice repeating the letter by tracing over each prompt.

k

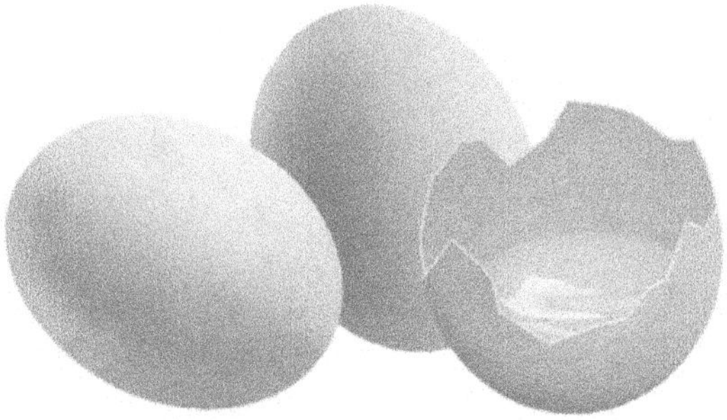

kai

[Egg]

First, trace following the directions; then repeat on the other prompts.

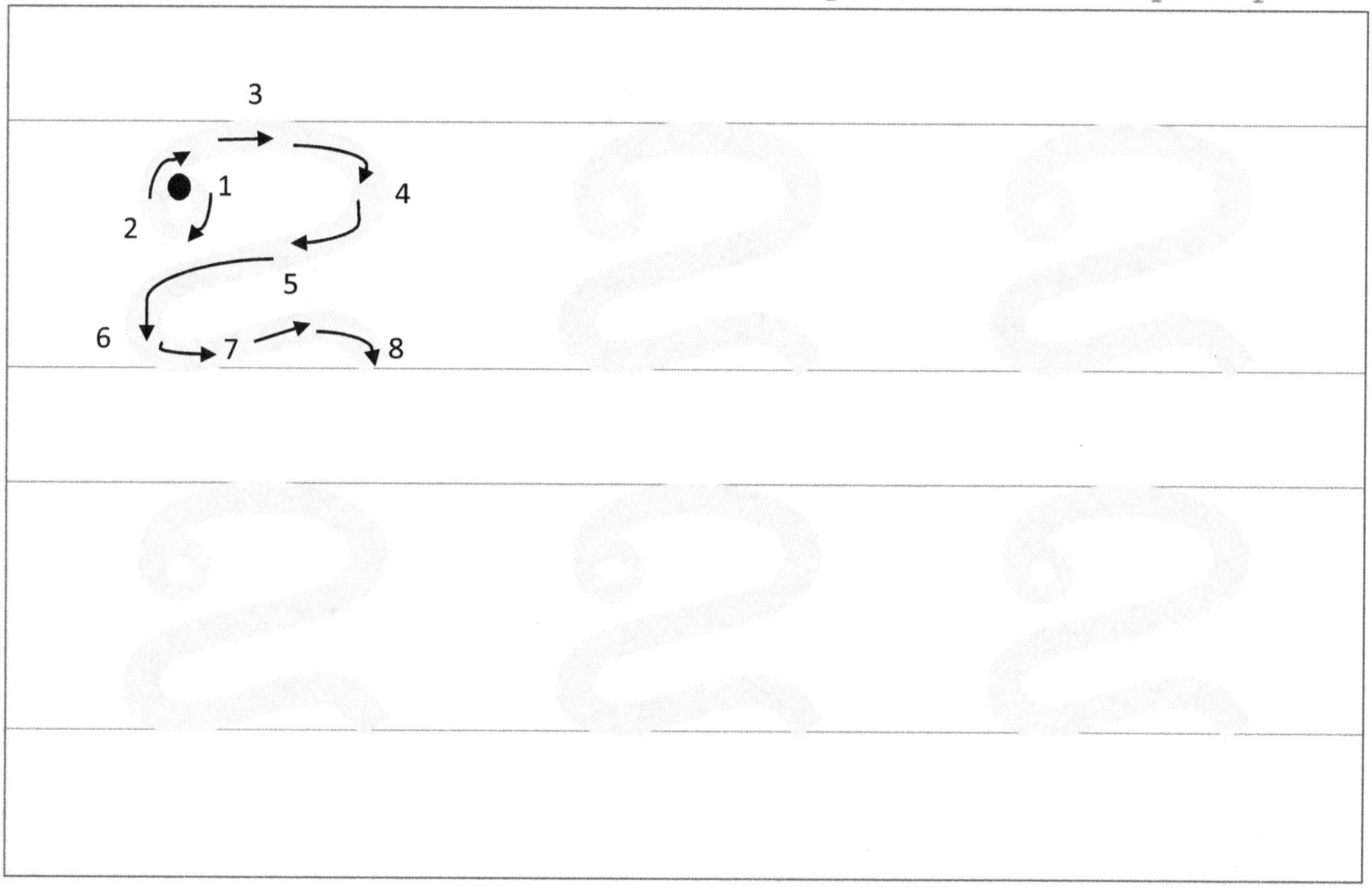

Practice repeating the letter by tracing over each prompt.

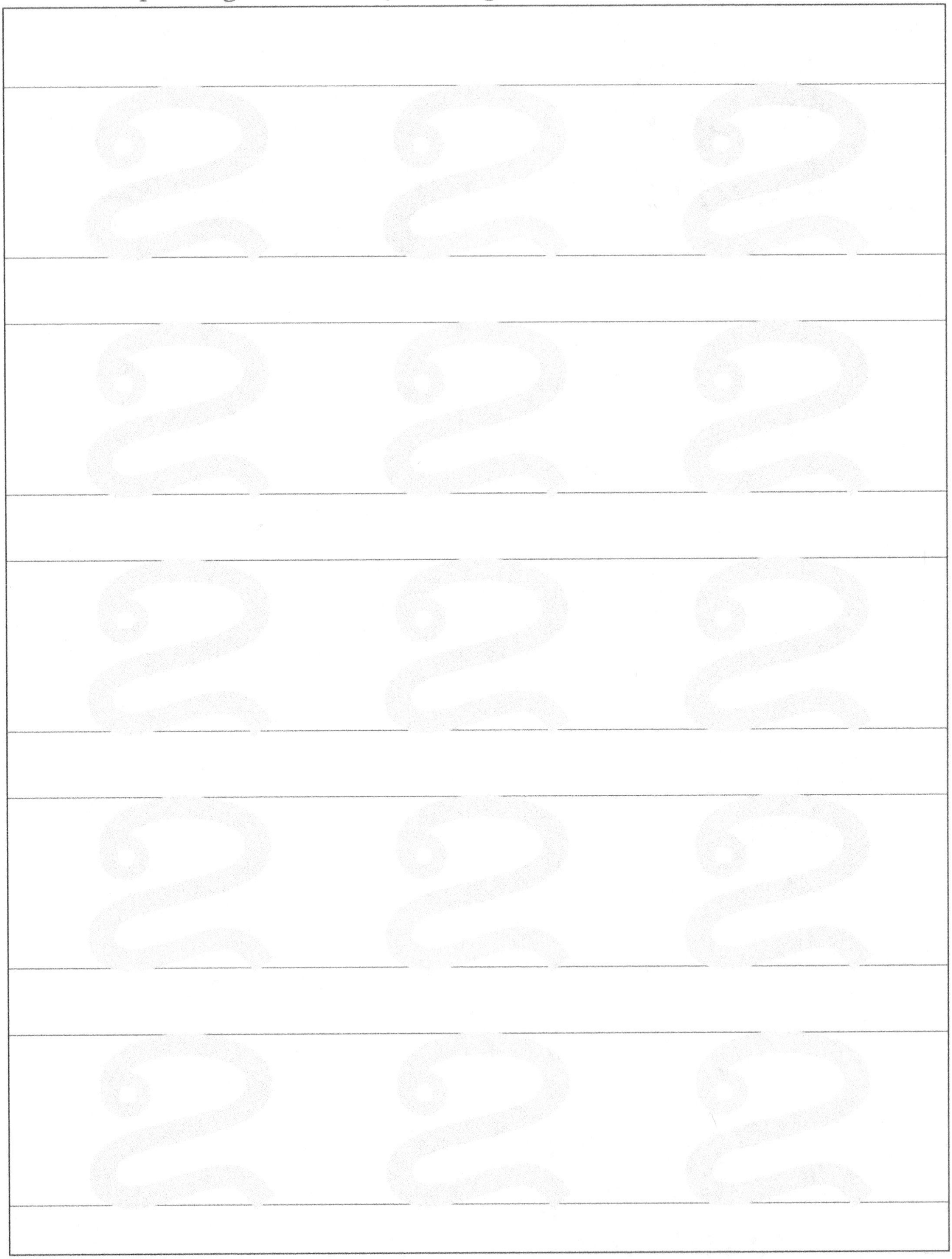

Practice repeating the letter by tracing over each prompt.

Practice repeating the letter by tracing over each prompt.

k

ຄວາຍ

kuaai

[Buffalo]

First, trace following the directions; then repeat on the other prompts.

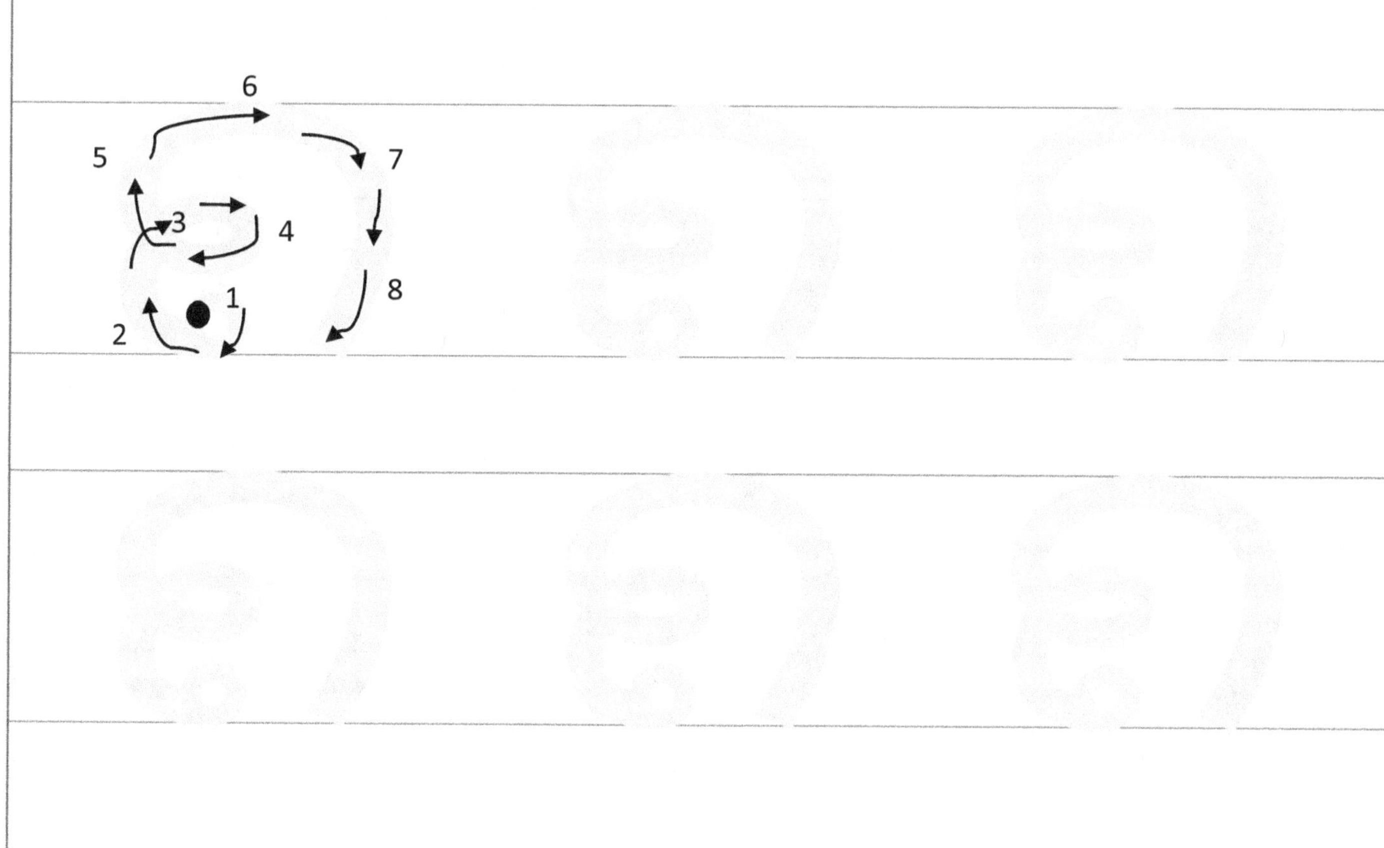

Practice repeating the letter by tracing over each prompt.

Practice repeating the letter by tracing over each prompt.

Practice repeating the letter by tracing over each prompt.

ng

ງໍ

ngua

[Cattle]

First, trace following the directions; then repeat on the other prompts.

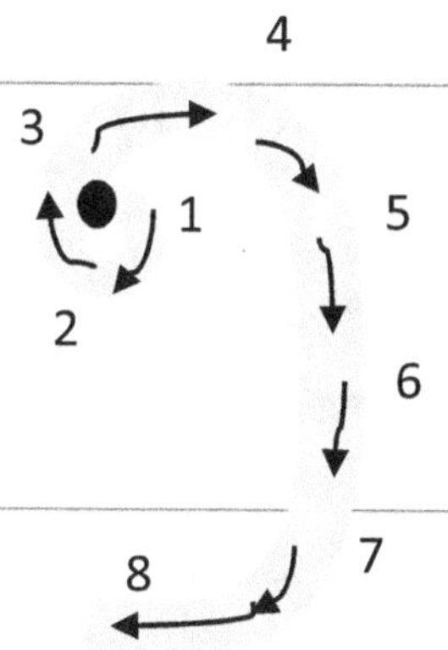

4

3

1

5

2

6

8   7

Practice repeating the letter by tracing over each prompt.

Practice repeating the letter by tracing over each prompt.

Practice repeating the letter by tracing over each prompt.

J

jawk

[Cup]

ຈອກ

First, trace following the directions; then repeat on the other prompts.

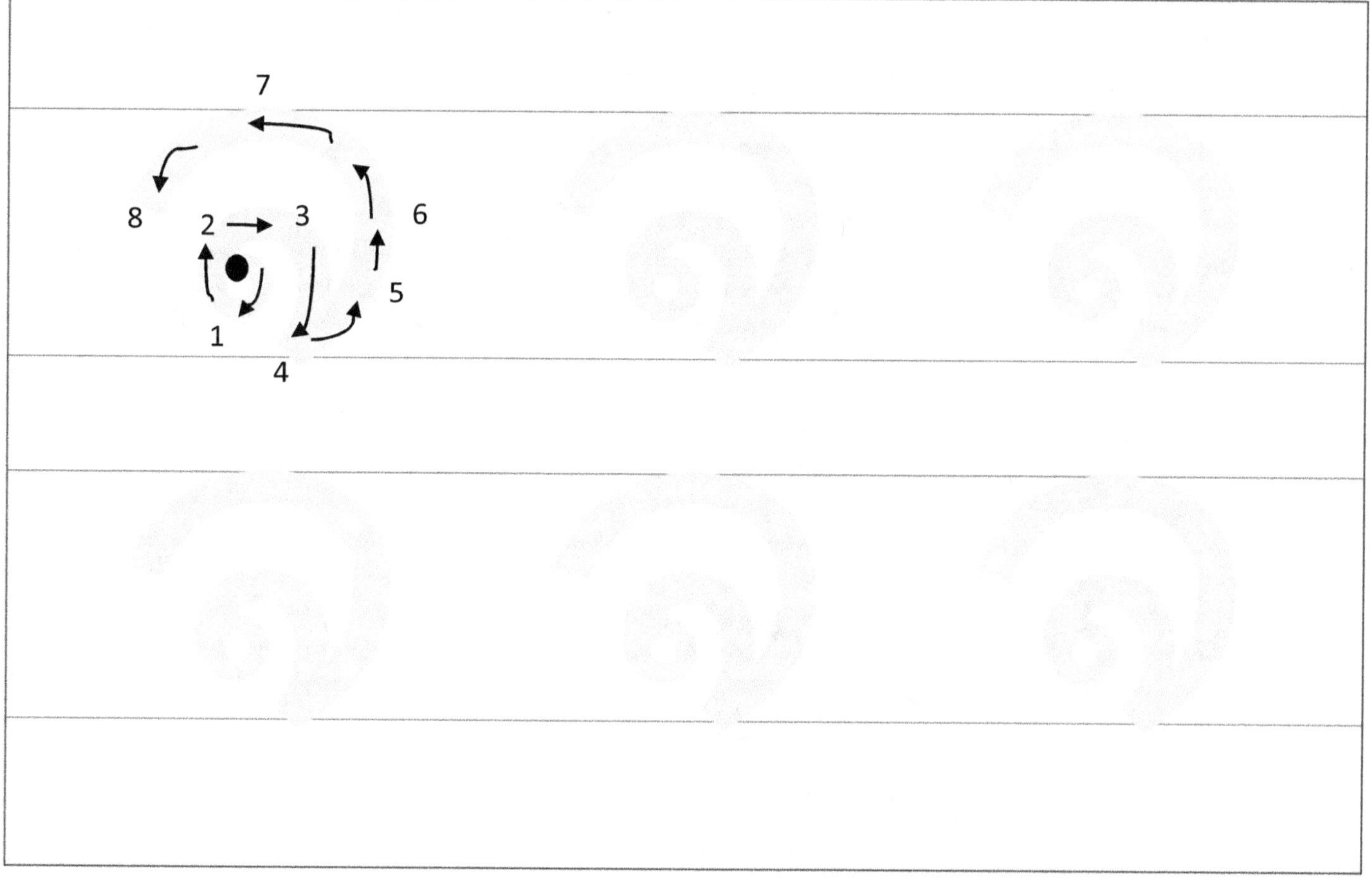

7
8   2 3   6
    1   5
      4

Practice repeating the letter by tracing over each prompt.

Practice repeating the letter by tracing over each prompt.

Practice repeating the letter by tracing over each prompt.

s

ເສືອ

seua

[Tiger]

First, trace following the directions; then repeat on the other prompts.

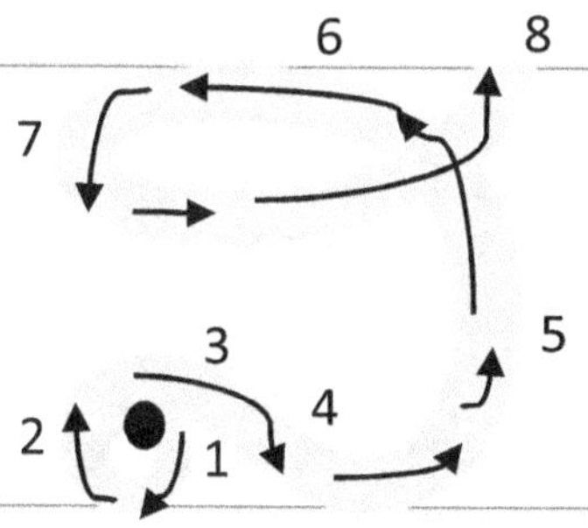

Practice repeating the letter by tracing over each prompt.

Practice repeating the letter by tracing over each prompt.

Practice repeating the letter by tracing over each prompt.

s

ช้าง

sang

[Elephant]

First, trace following the directions; then repeat on the other prompts.

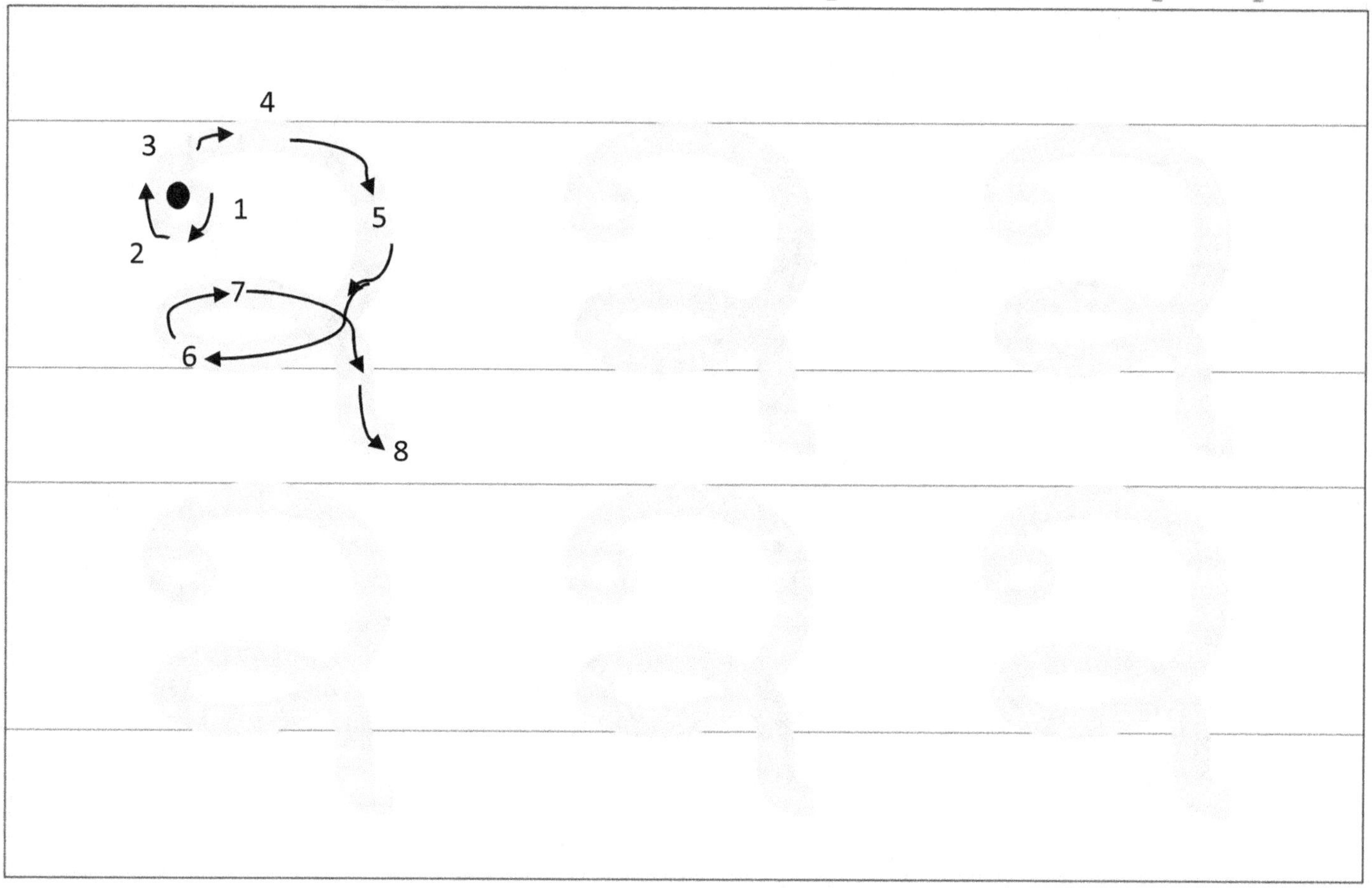

Practice repeating the letter by tracing over each prompt.

Practice repeating the letter by tracing over each prompt.

Practice repeating the letter by tracing over each prompt.

ny

ຍ຺ງ

nyung

[Mosquito]

First, trace following the directions; then repeat on the other prompts.

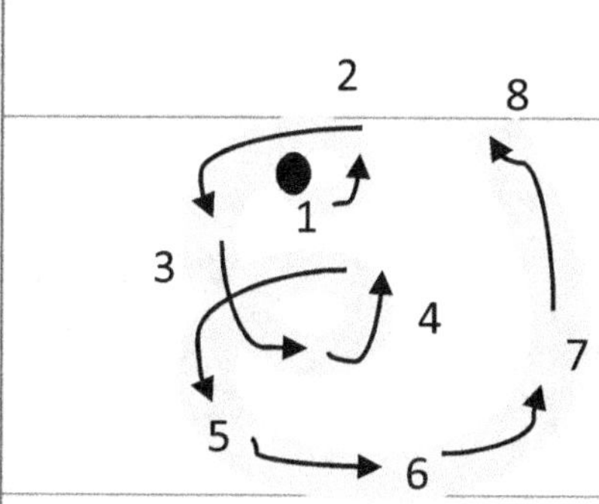

Practice repeating the letter by tracing over each prompt.

Practice repeating the letter by tracing over each prompt.

Practice repeating the letter by tracing over each prompt.

d

เด็ก

dek

[kid]

First, trace following the directions; then repeat on the other prompts.

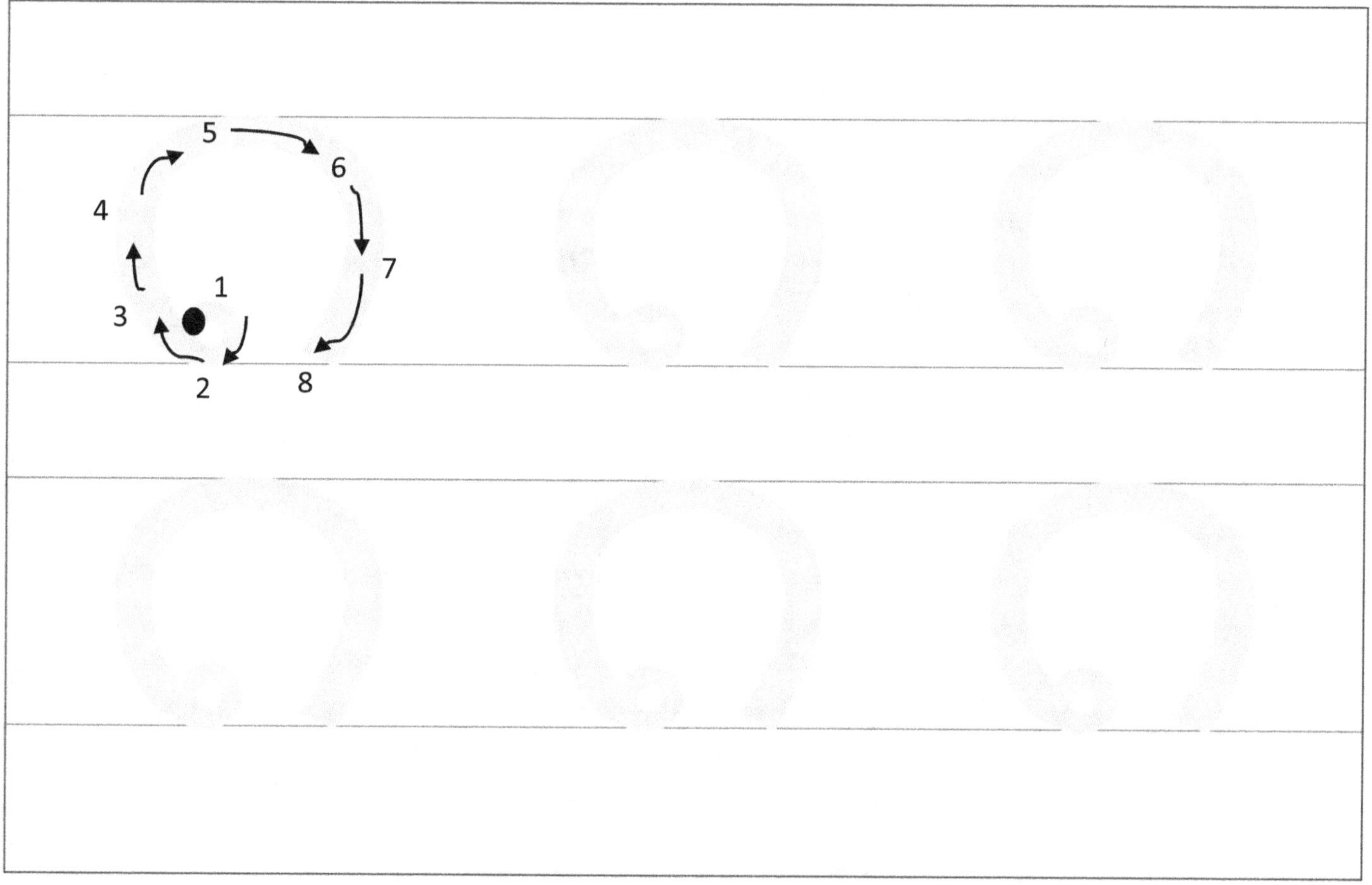

Practice repeating the letter by tracing over each prompt.

Practice repeating the letter by tracing over each prompt.

Practice repeating the letter by tracing over each prompt.

dt

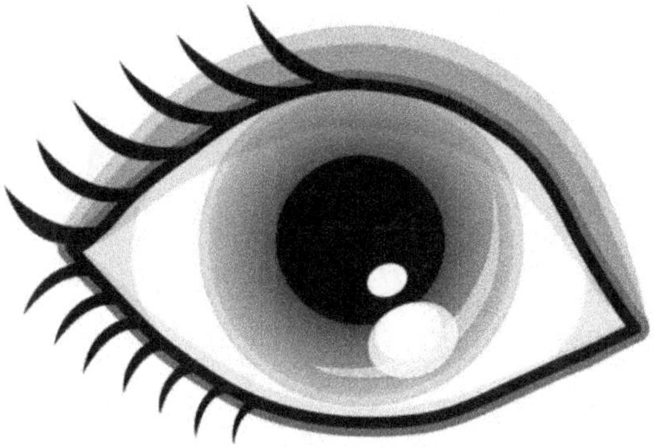

ങ

dtaa

[eye]

First, trace following the directions; then repeat on the other prompts.

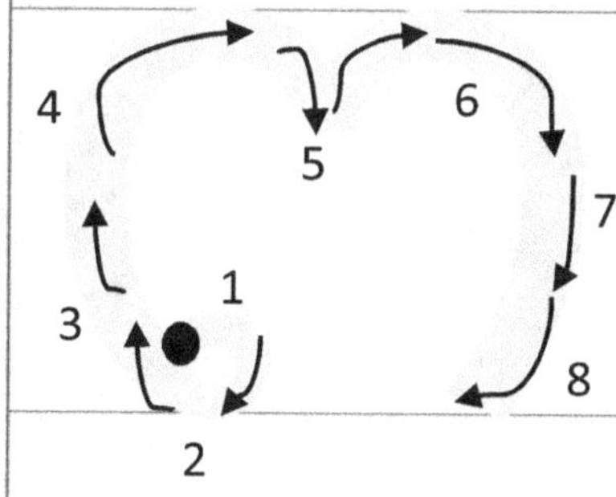

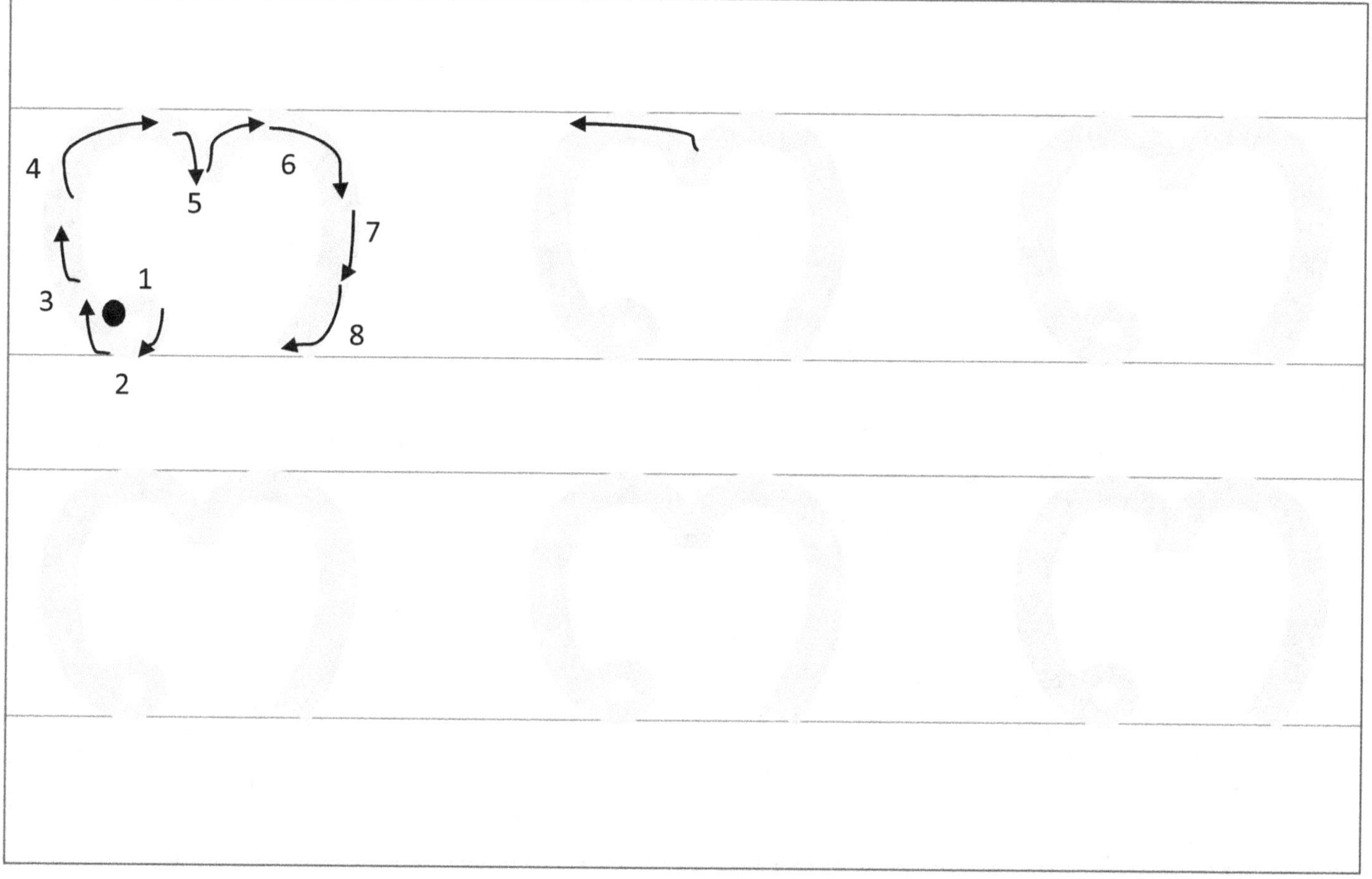

Practice repeating the letter by tracing over each prompt.

Practice repeating the letter by tracing over each prompt.

Practice repeating the letter by tracing over each prompt.

ก

t

ถุง

tong

[Bag]

First, trace following the directions; then repeat on the other prompts.

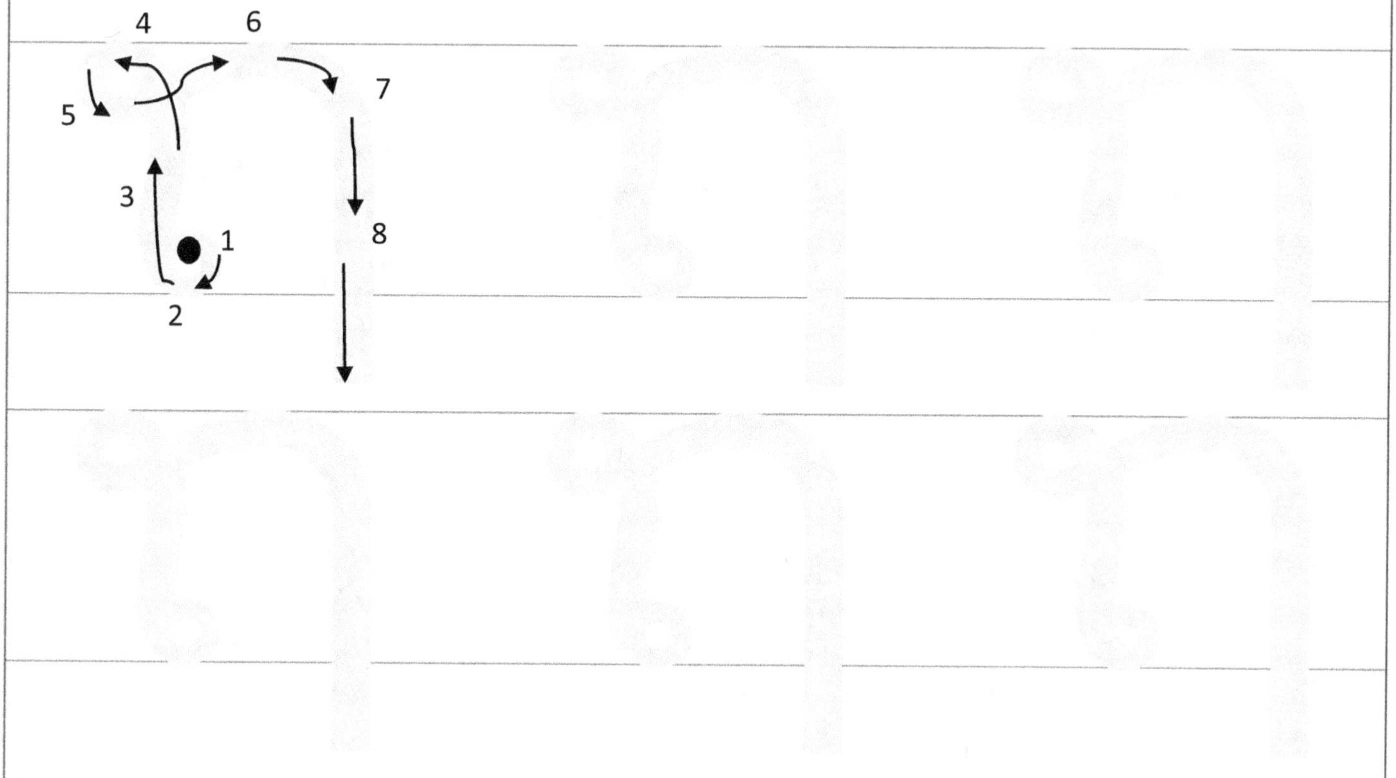

Practice repeating the letter by tracing over each prompt.

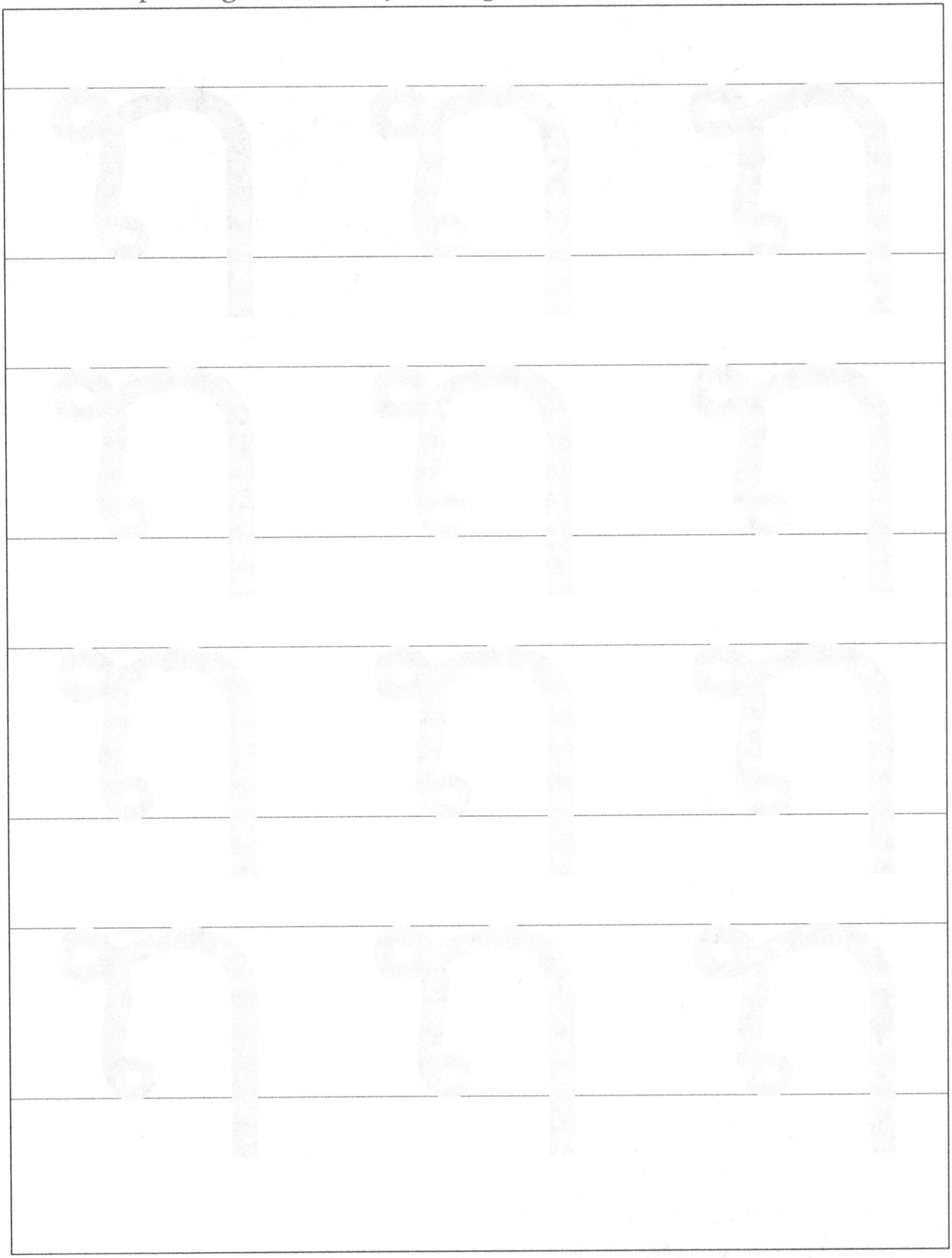

Practice repeating the letter by tracing over each prompt.

Practice repeating the letter by tracing over each prompt.

ທ

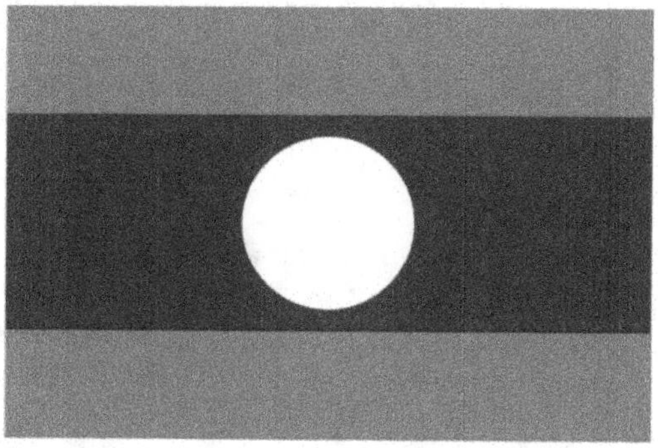

t

tung

ທຸງ

[Flag]

First, trace following the directions; then repeat on the other prompts.

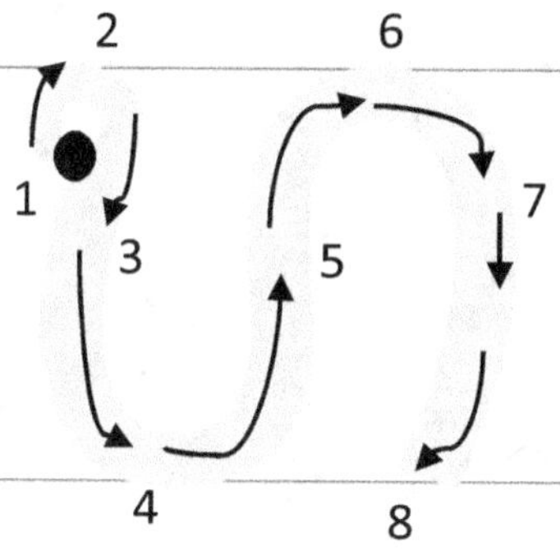

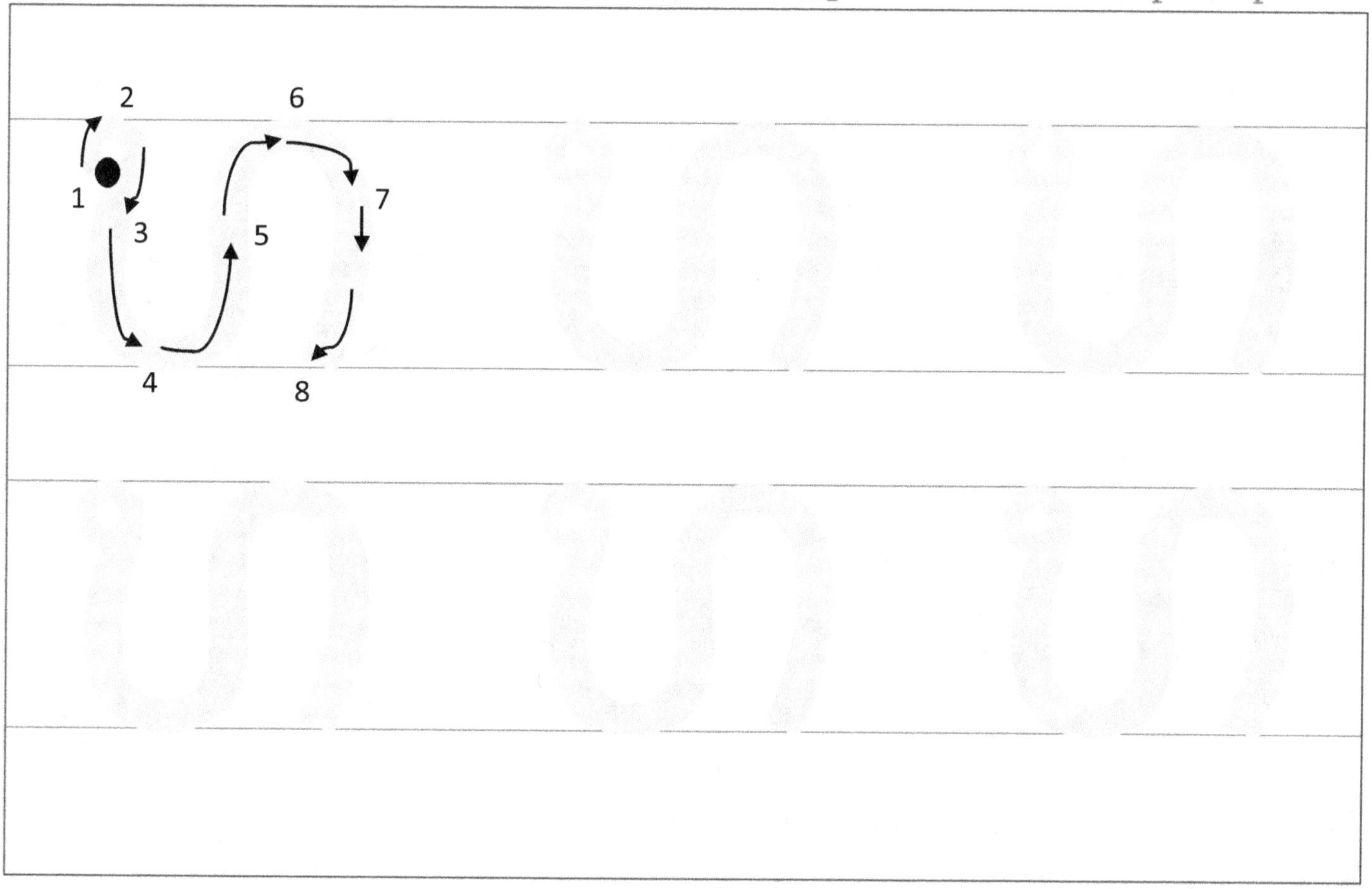

Practice repeating the letter by tracing over each prompt.

Practice repeating the letter by tracing over each prompt.

Practice repeating the letter by tracing over each prompt.

ນ

n

ນົກ

nok

[Bird]

First, trace following the directions; then repeat on the other prompts.

Practice repeating the letter by tracing over each prompt.

Practice repeating the letter by tracing over each prompt.

Practice repeating the letter by tracing over each prompt.

b

ccُ

baae

[Goat]

First, trace following the directions; then repeat on the other prompts.

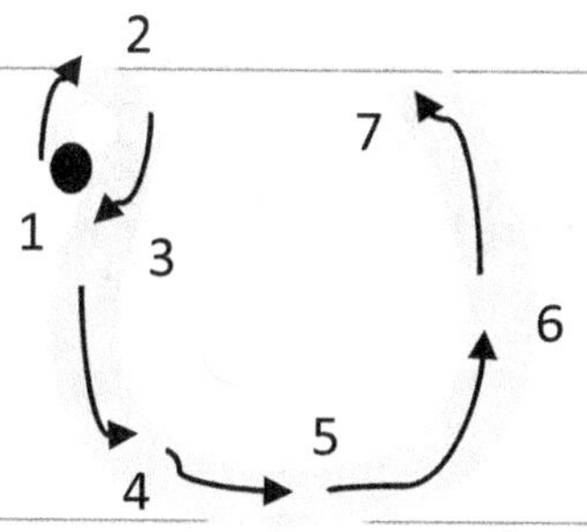

Practice repeating the letter by tracing over each prompt.

Practice repeating the letter by tracing over each prompt.

Practice repeating the letter by tracing over each prompt.

bp

bpaa

บ า

[Fish]

First, trace following the directions; then repeat on the other prompts.

Practice repeating the letter by tracing over each prompt.

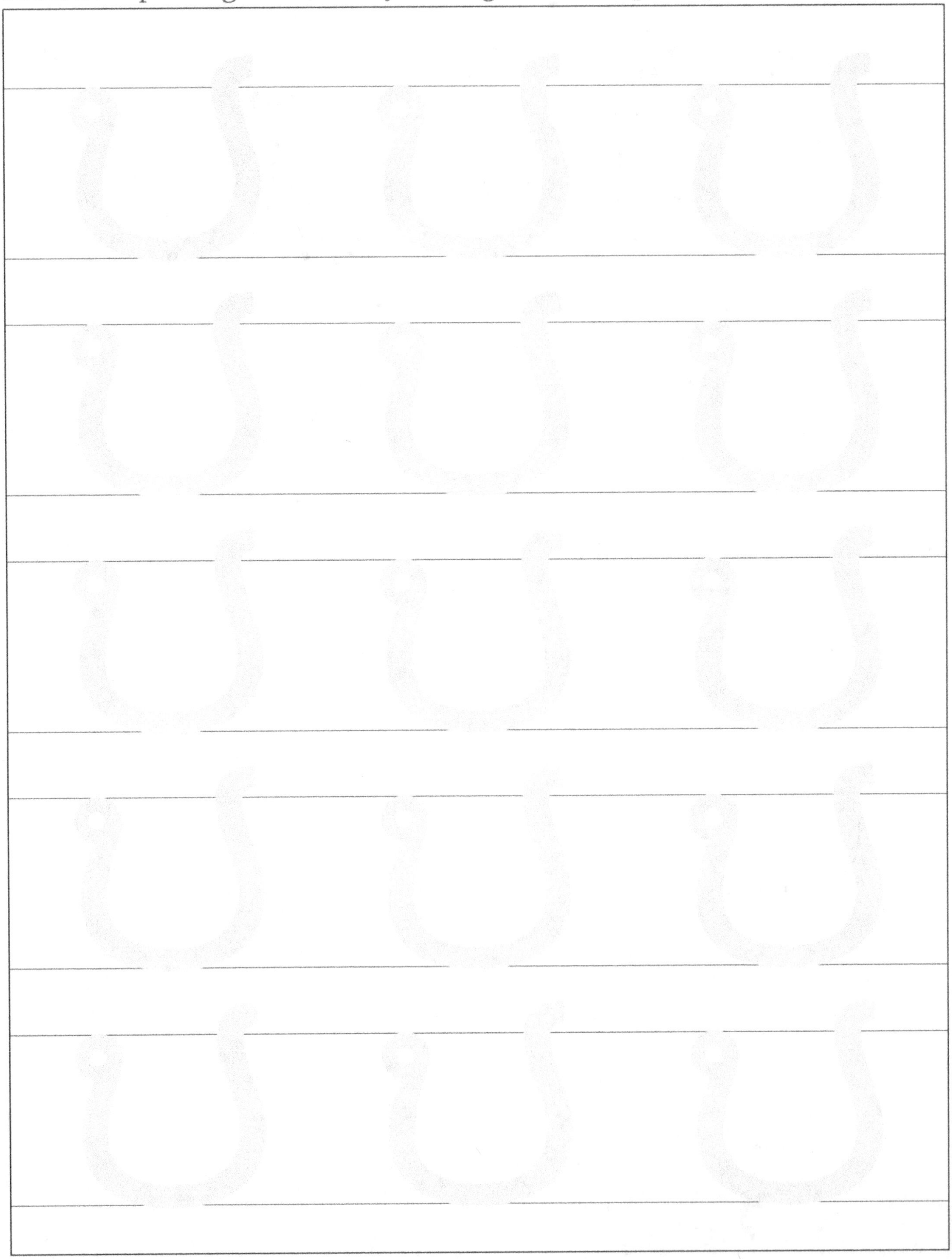

Practice repeating the letter by tracing over each prompt.

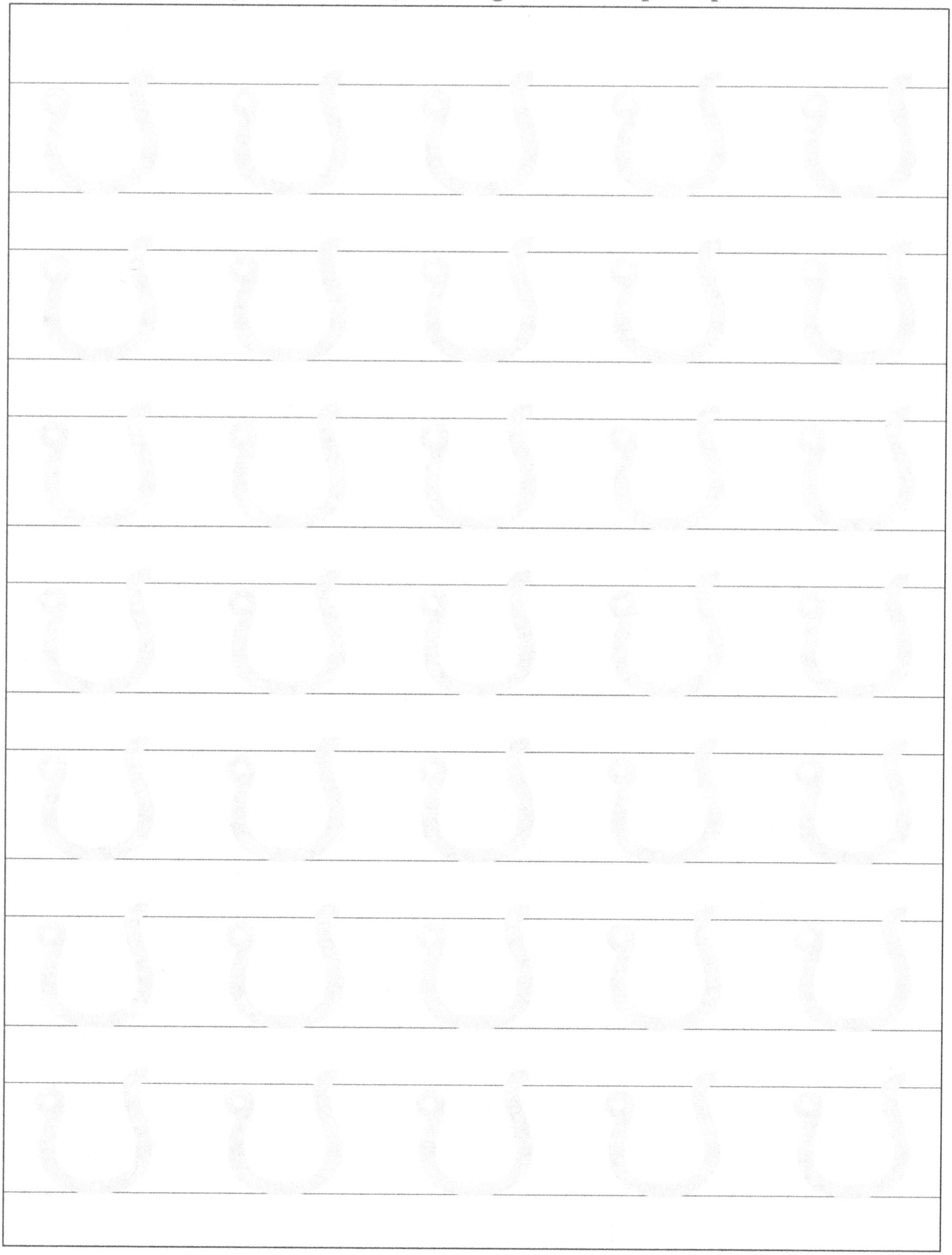

Practice repeating the letter by tracing over each prompt.

p

ဗ

[perrn]...

perrn

[Bee]

First, trace following the directions; then repeat on the other prompts.

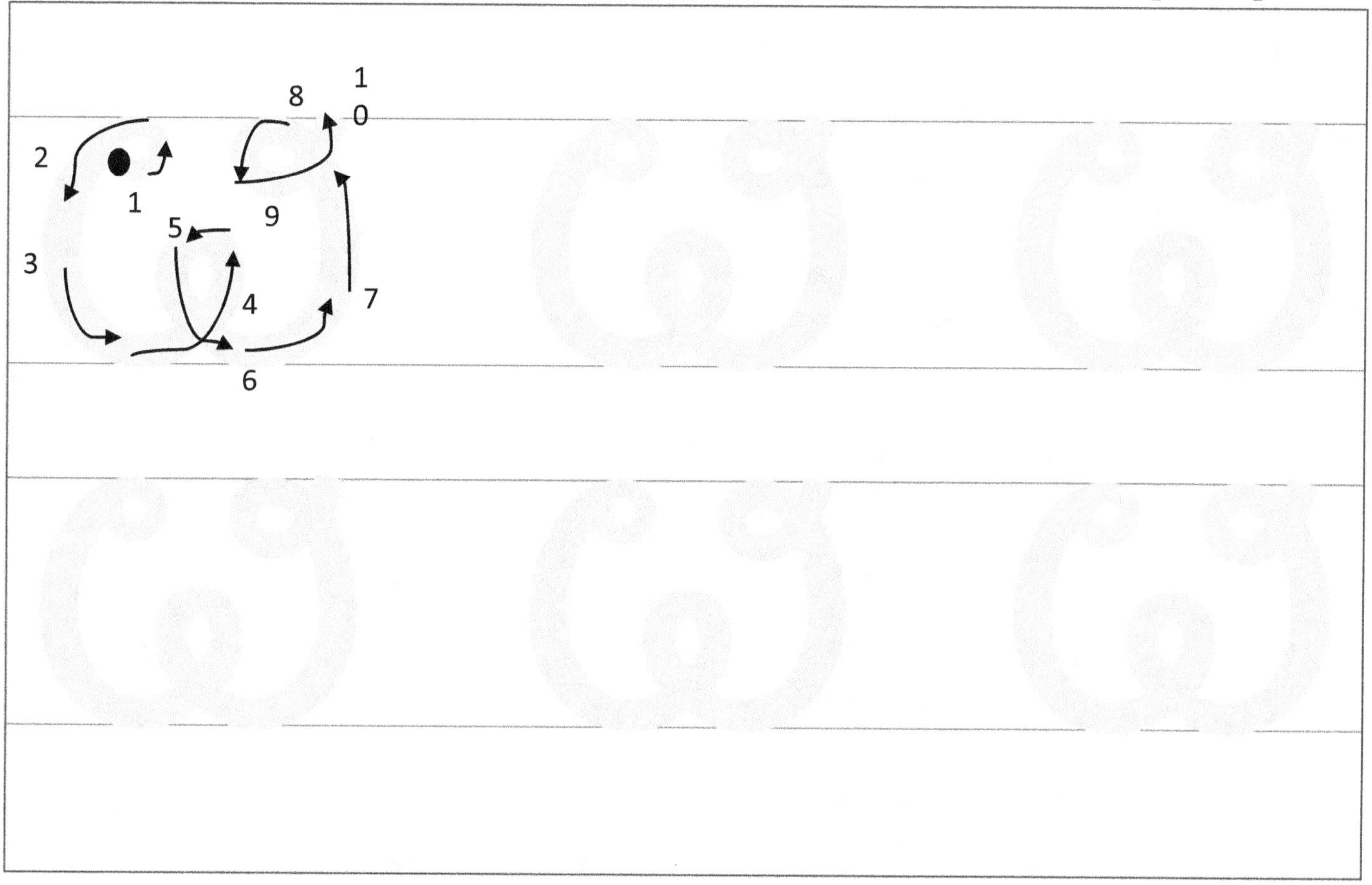

Practice repeating the letter by tracing over each prompt.

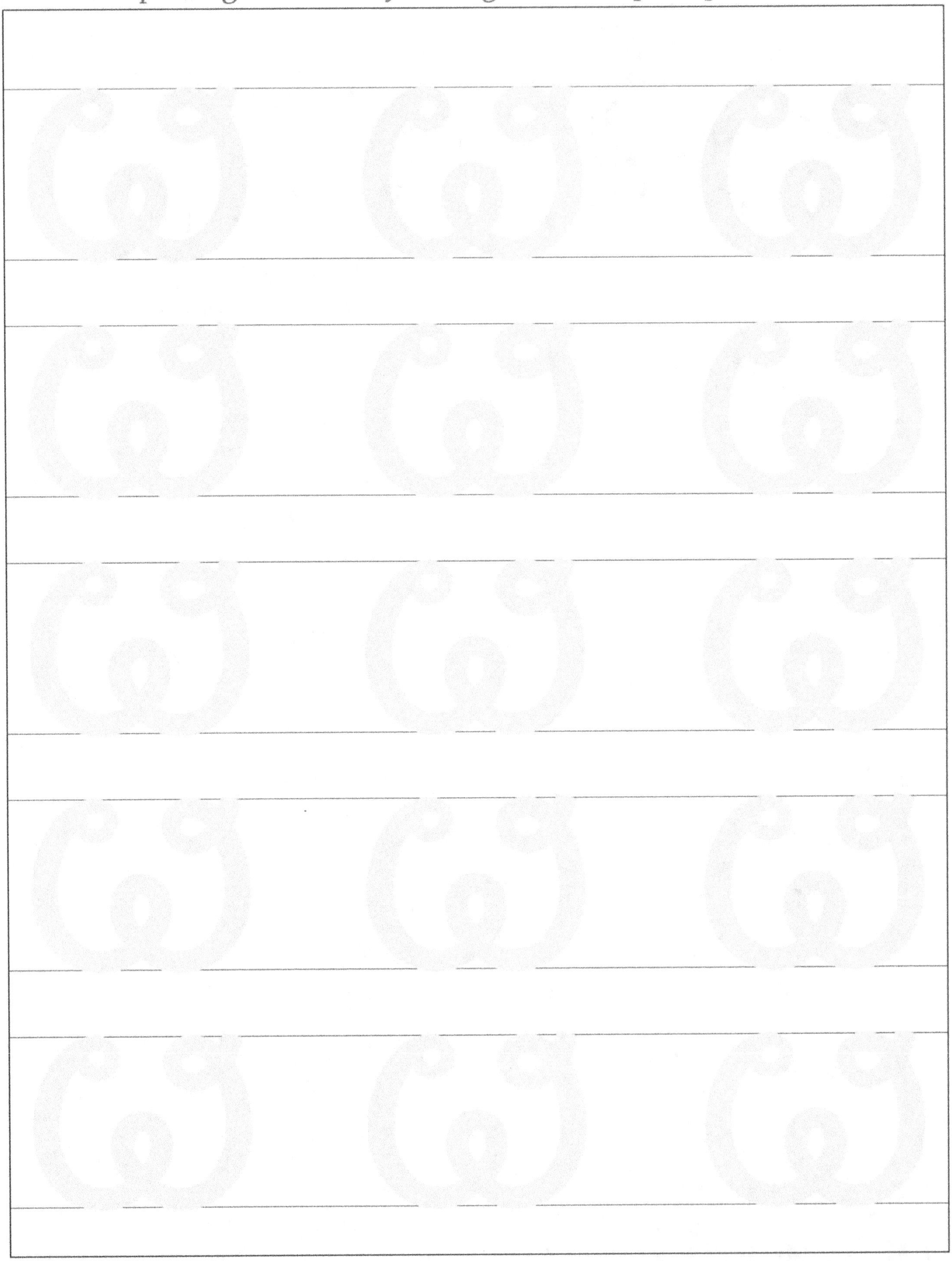

Practice repeating the letter by tracing over each prompt.

Practice repeating the letter by tracing over each prompt.

f

ฝิน

fon

[Rain]

First, trace following the directions; then repeat on the other prompts.

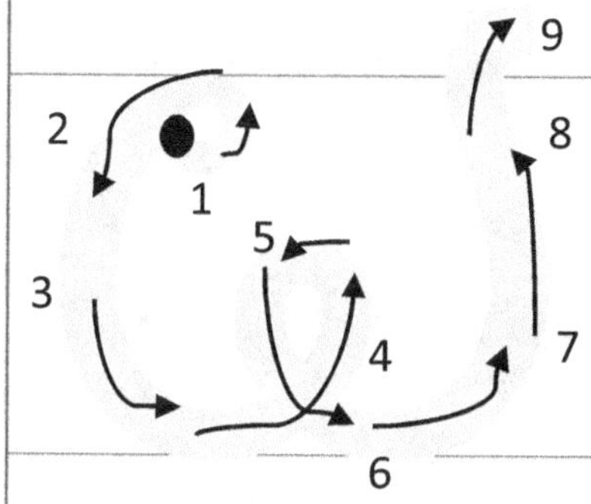

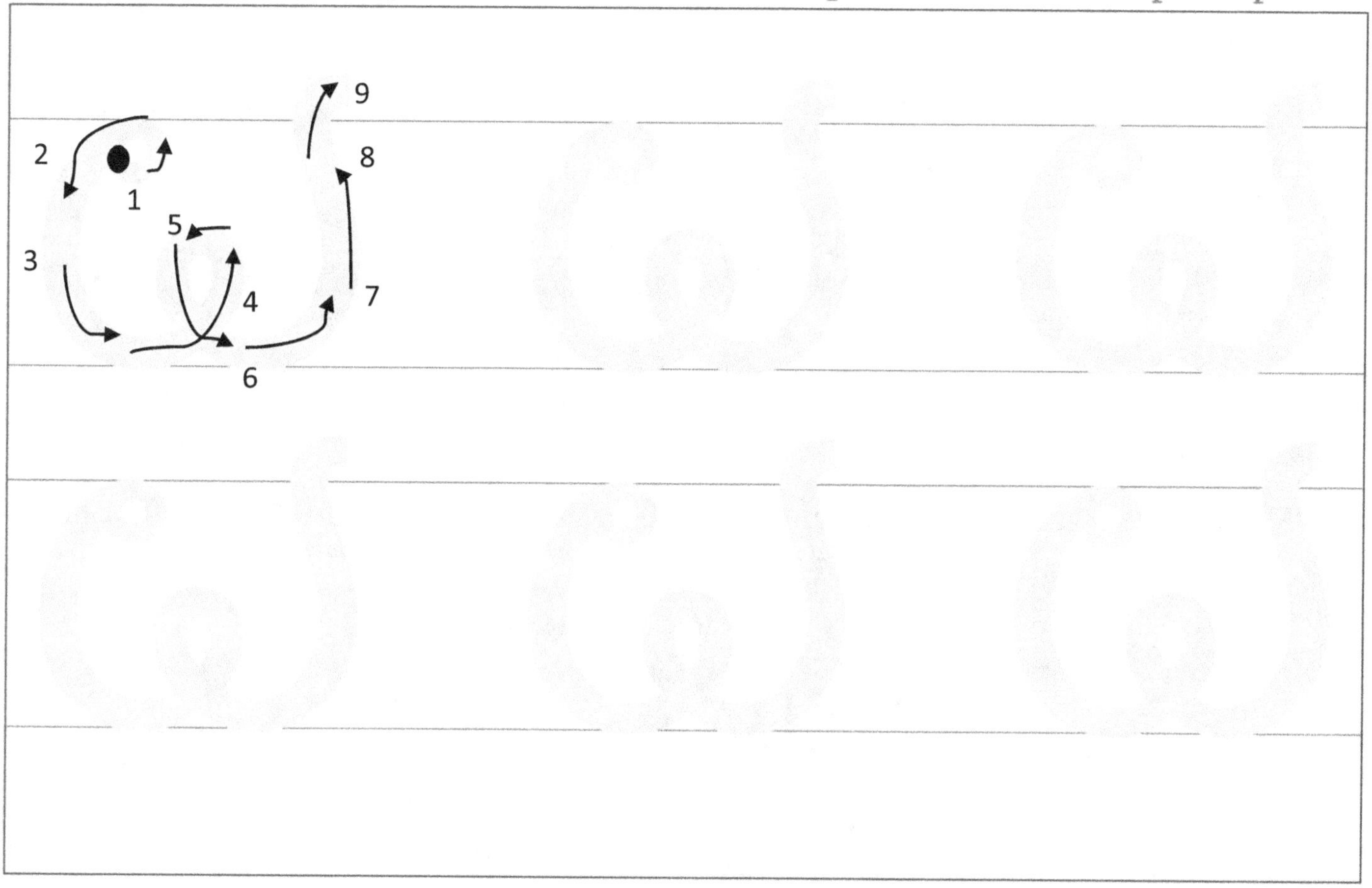

Practice repeating the letter by tracing over each prompt.

Practice repeating the letter by tracing over each prompt.

Practice repeating the letter by tracing over each prompt.

ph

ڛ

puu

[Mountain]

First, trace following the directions; then repeat on the other prompts.

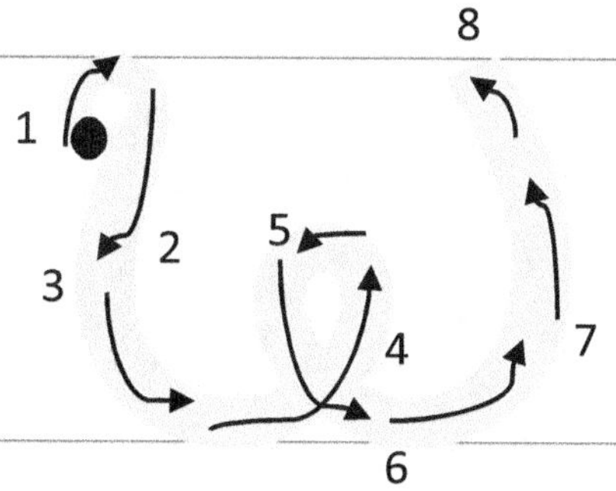

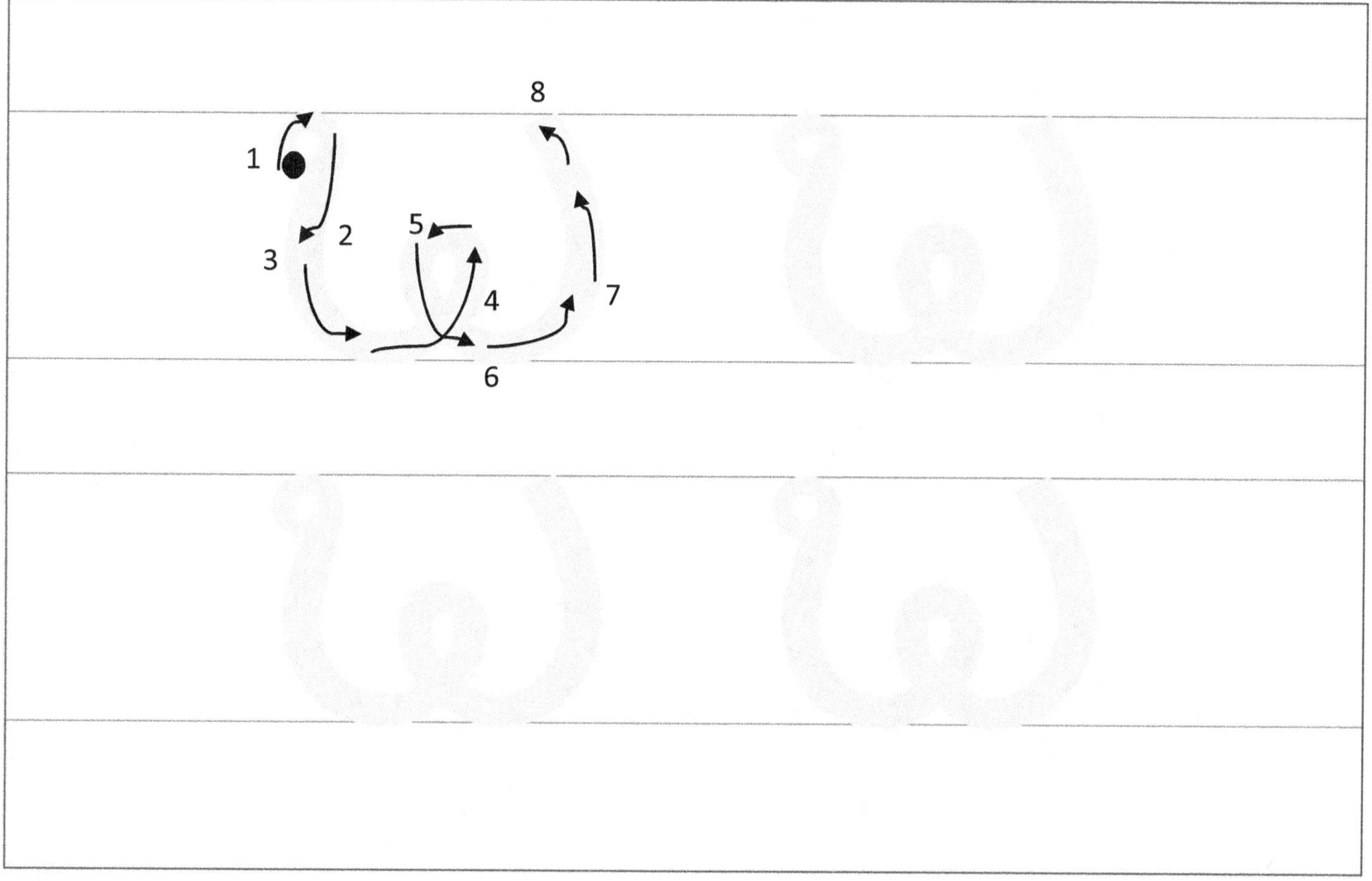

Practice repeating the letter by tracing over each prompt.

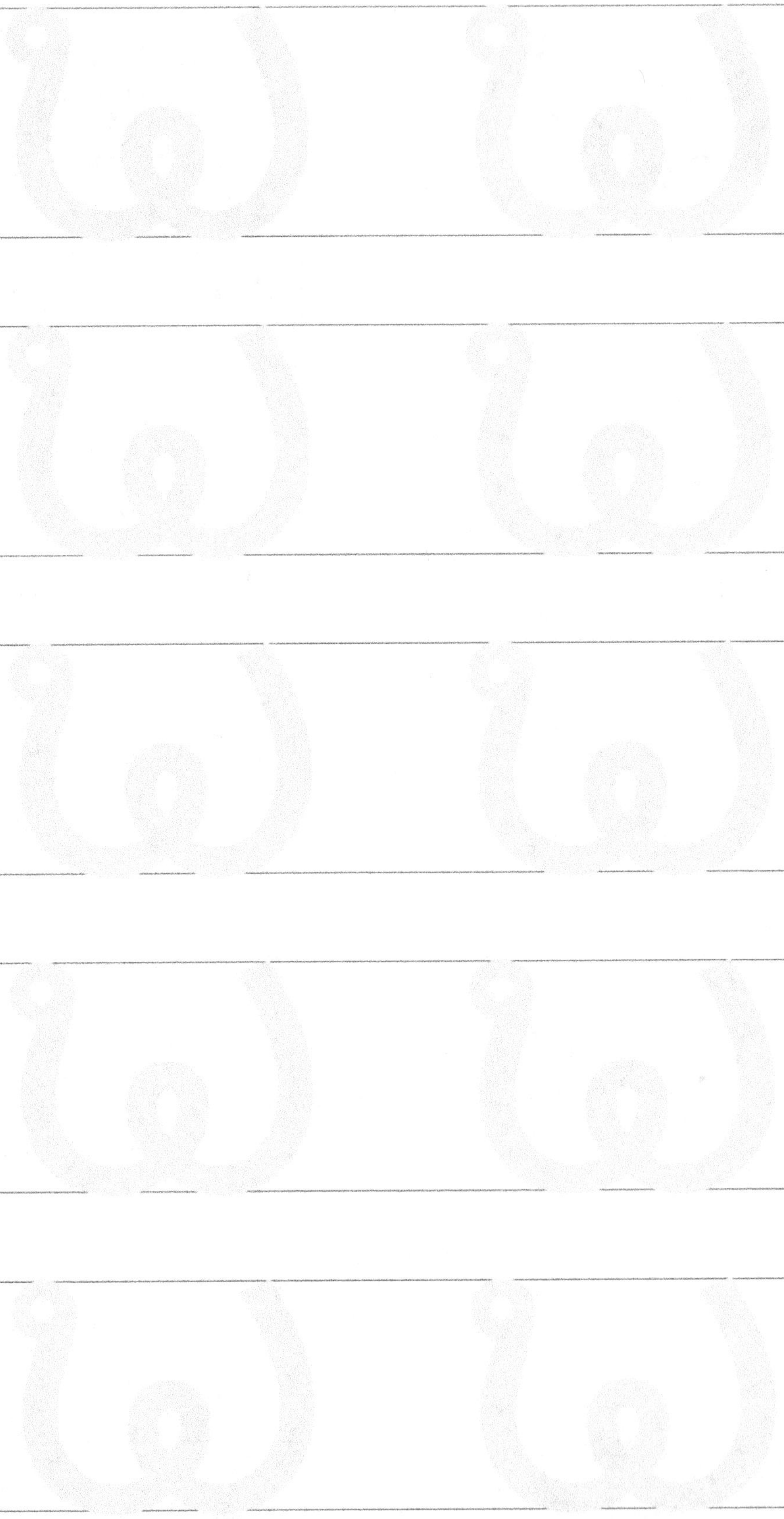

Practice repeating the letter by tracing over each prompt.

Practice repeating the letter by tracing over each prompt.

ຟ

f

ໄຟ

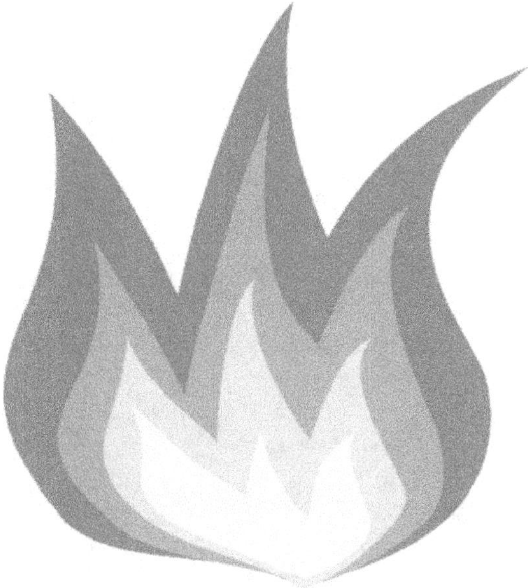

fai

[Fire]

First, trace following the directions; then repeat on the other prompts.

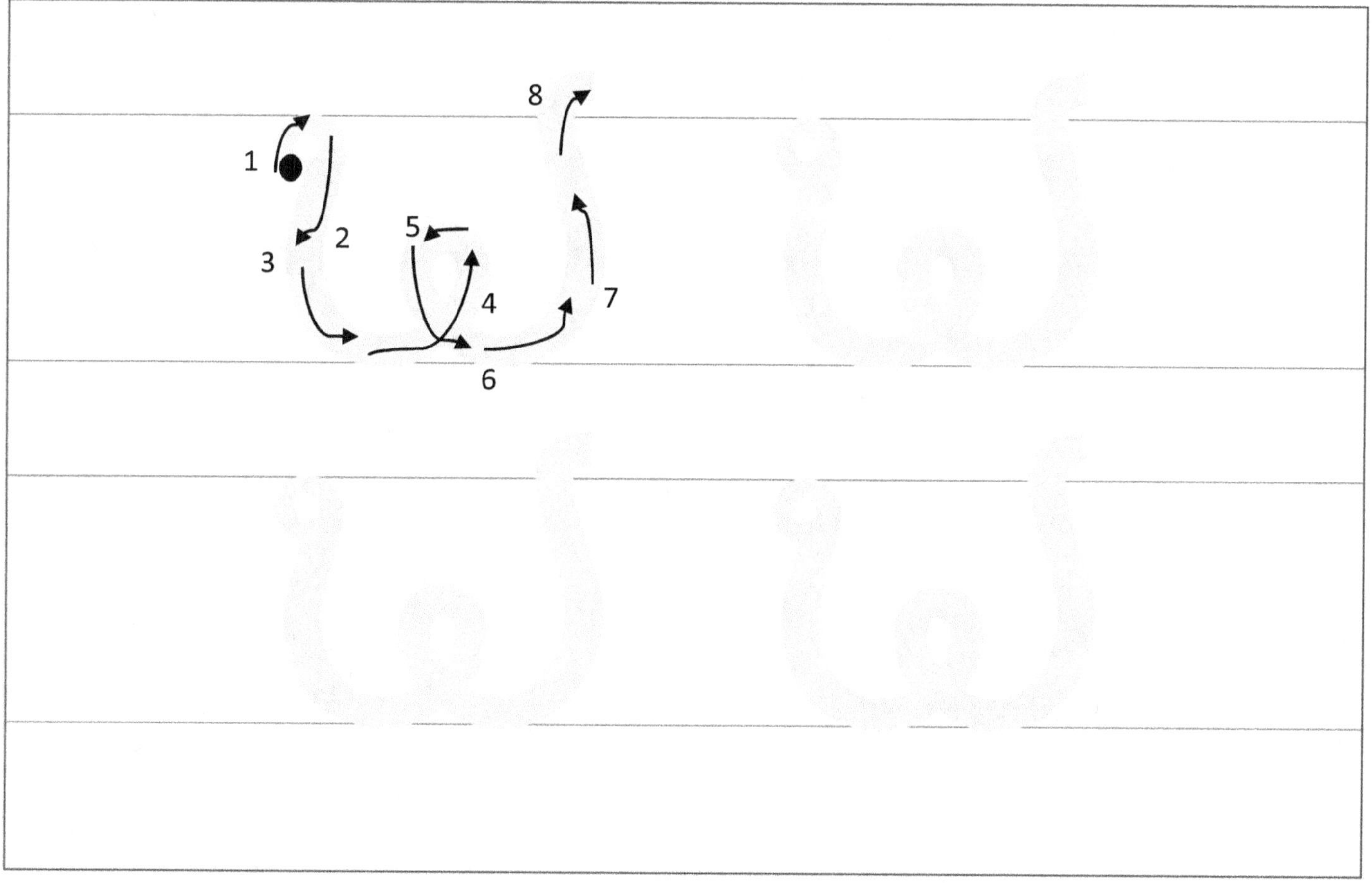

Practice repeating the letter by tracing over each prompt.

Practice repeating the letter by tracing over each prompt.

Practice repeating the letter by tracing over each prompt.

ມ

m

ມ້າ

ma

[Horse]

First, trace following the directions; then repeat on the other prompts.

Practice repeating the letter by tracing over each prompt.

Practice repeating the letter by tracing over each prompt.

Practice repeating the letter by tracing over each prompt.

ຍ

y

ຍາ

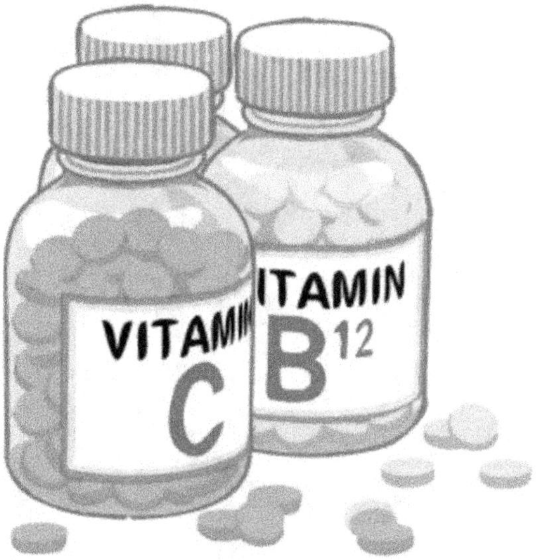

yaa

[Medicine]

First, trace following the directions; then repeat on the other prompts.

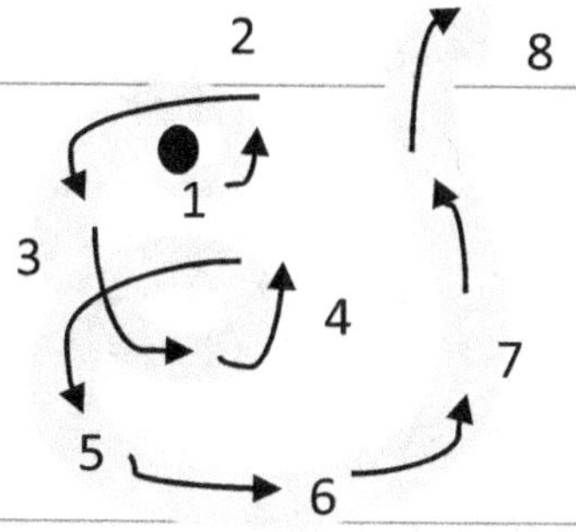

Practice repeating the letter by tracing over each prompt.

Practice repeating the letter by tracing over each prompt.

Practice repeating the letter by tracing over each prompt.

ລ

l

ລີງ

leeng

[Monkey]

First, trace following the directions; then repeat on the other prompts.

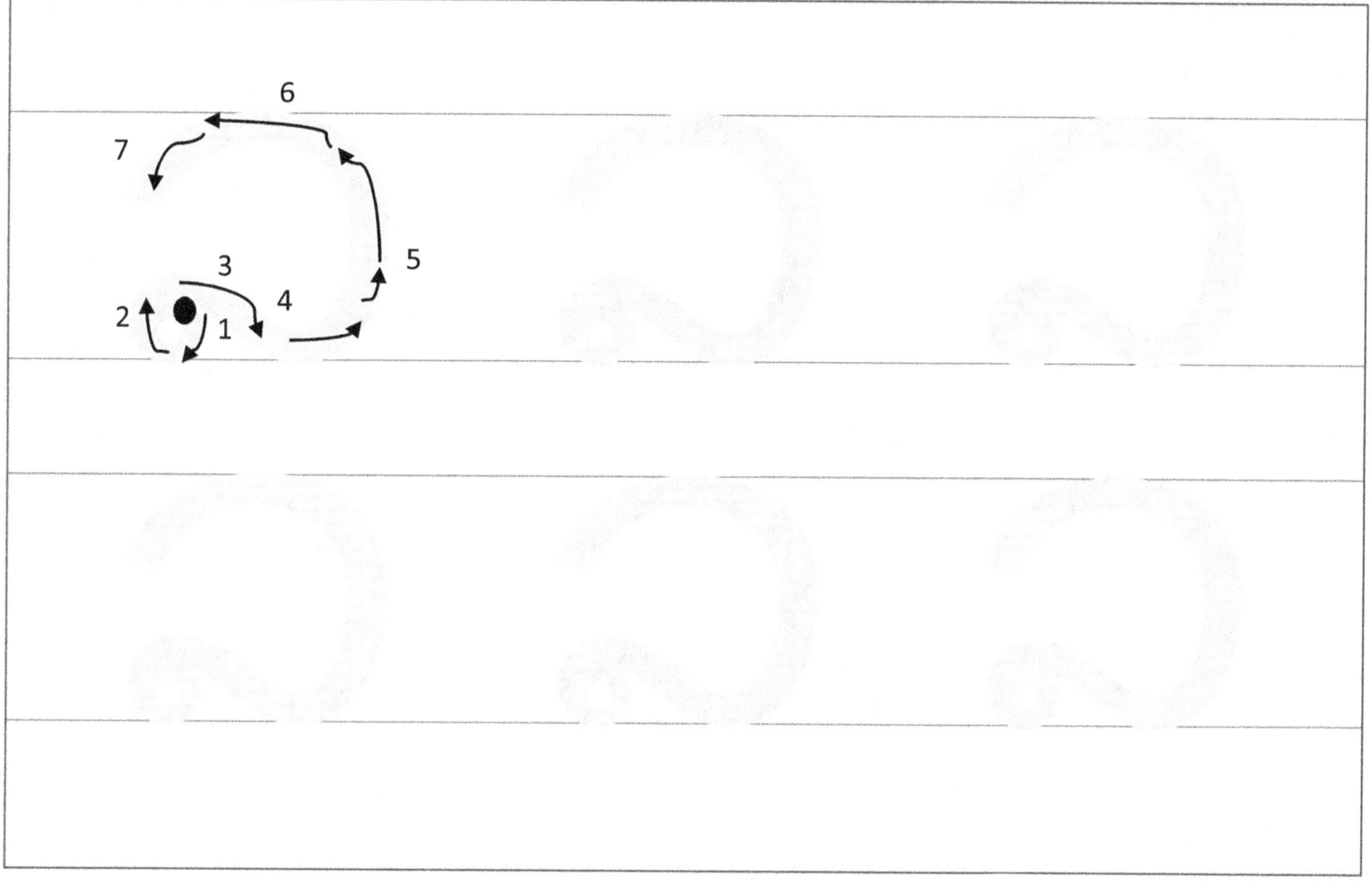

Practice repeating the letter by tracing over each prompt.

Practice repeating the letter by tracing over each prompt.

Practice repeating the letter by tracing over each prompt.

V

vee

[Fan]

First, trace following the directions; then repeat on the other prompts.

7 6
8
5
2
1 4
3

Practice repeating the letter by tracing over each prompt.

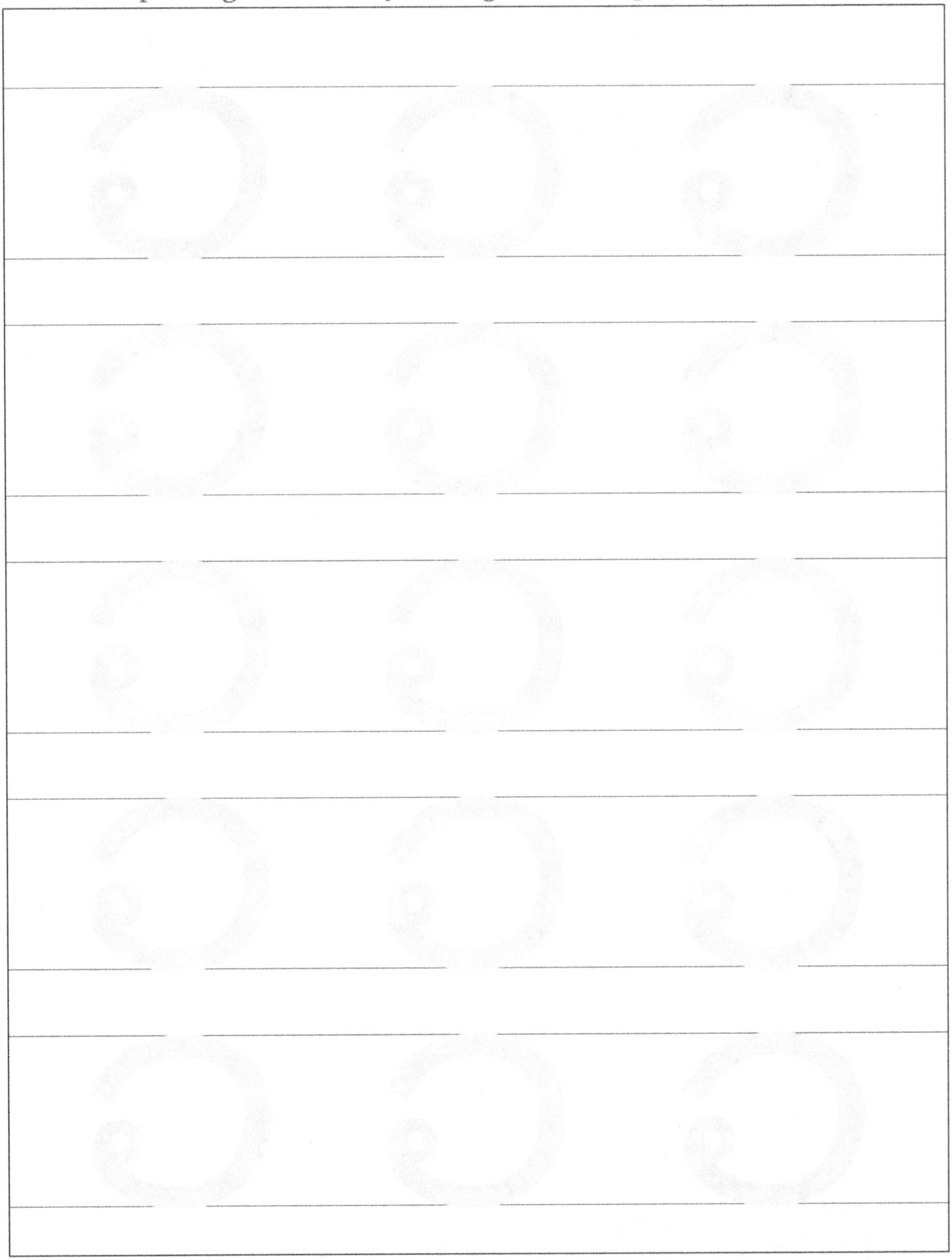

Practice repeating the letter by tracing over each prompt.

Practice repeating the letter by tracing over each prompt.

ຫ

h

ຫ່ານ

haan

[Goose]

First, trace following the directions; then repeat on the other prompts.

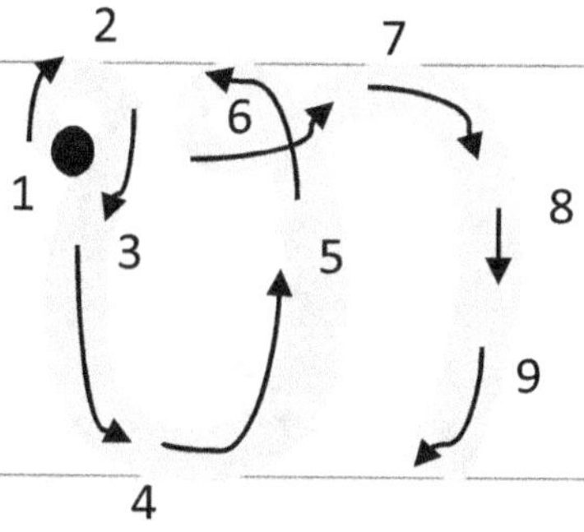

Practice repeating the letter by tracing over each prompt.

Practice repeating the letter by tracing over each prompt.

Practice repeating the letter by tracing over each prompt.

ອ

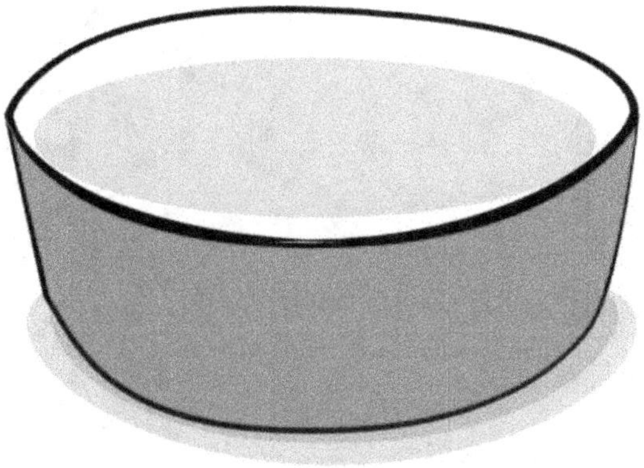

aw

oo

ໂອ

[Drinking Bowl]

First, trace following the directions; then repeat on the other prompts.

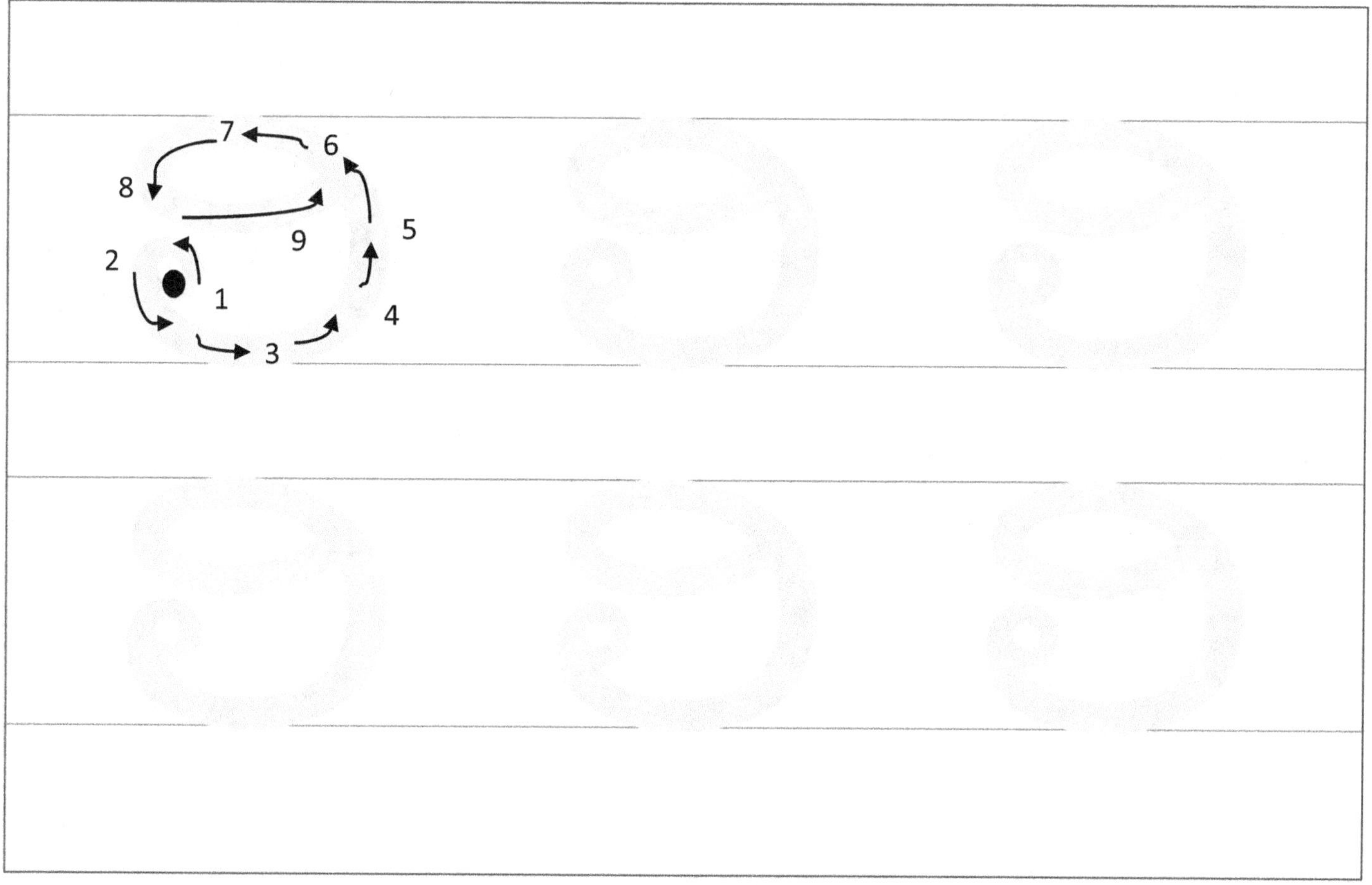

Practice repeating the letter by tracing over each prompt.

Practice repeating the letter by tracing over each prompt.

Practice repeating the letter by tracing over each prompt.

ຣ

h

ເຮືອນ

heaun

[House]

First, trace following the directions; then repeat on the other prompts.

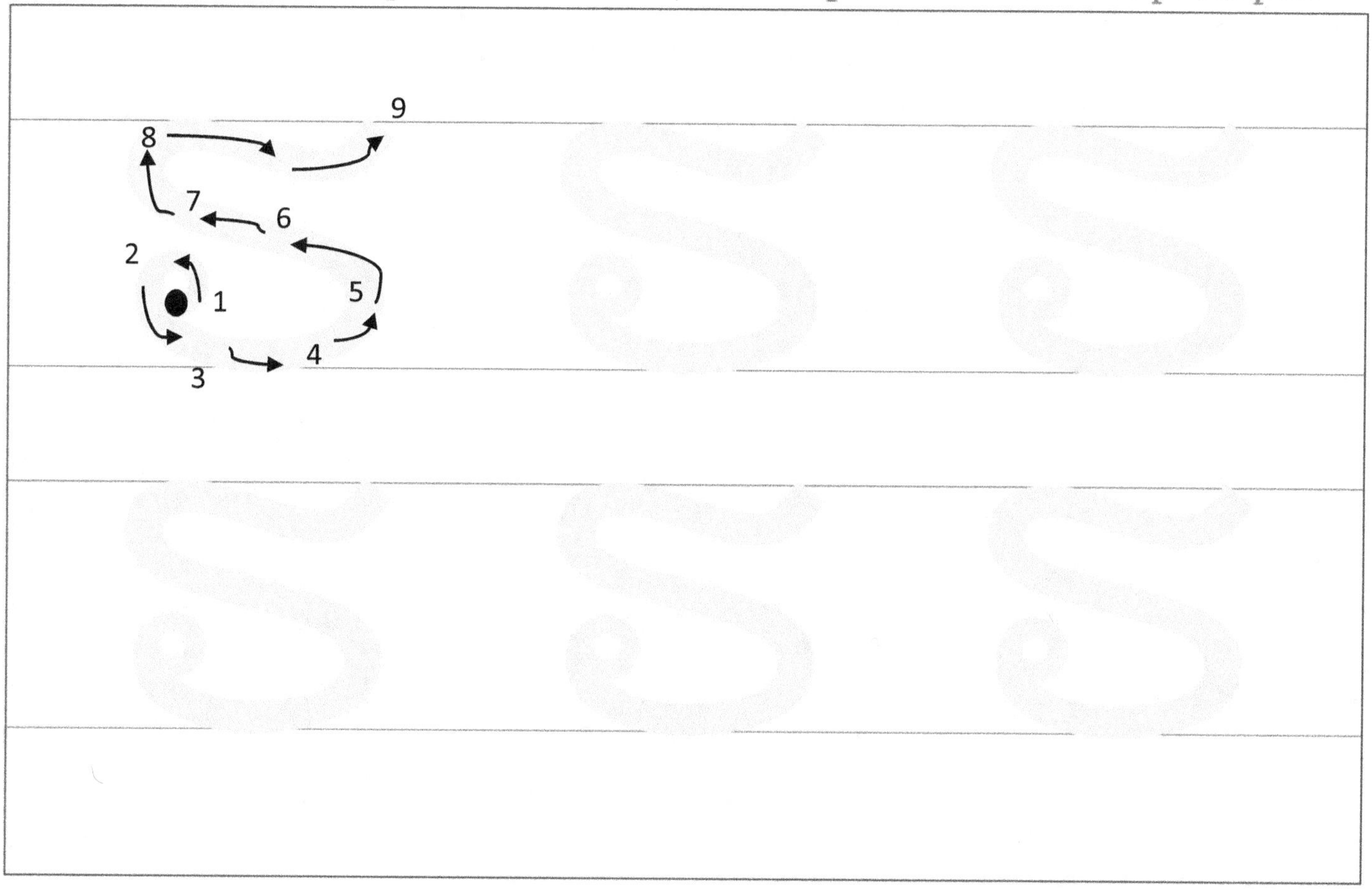

Practice repeating the letter by tracing over each prompt.

Practice repeating the letter by tracing over each prompt.

Practice repeating the letter by tracing over each prompt.

s

r

ระฅัງ

rakang

[Bell]

First, trace following the directions; then repeat on the other prompts.

Practice repeating the letter by tracing over each prompt.

Practice repeating the letter by tracing over each prompt.

Practice repeating the letter by tracing over each prompt.

Lao Consonants Alphabets/Letters

ພາສາລາວ

ກ ຂ ຄ ງ ຈ

ສ ຊ ຍ ດ ຕ

ຖ ທ ນ ບ ປ

ຜ ຝ ພ ຟ ມ

ຍ ຣ ລ ວ ຫ

ອ ຮ